The Sacred Love Letter

Krishna weds Rukmini

Kiran Java

The Krishna Series

Copyright © 2022 Kiran Java

All rights reserved

No part of this book may be reproduced, or stored in a retrieval system, or transmitted in any form or by any means, electronic, mechanical, photocopying, recording, or otherwise, without express written permission of the publisher.

www.kiranjava.com

*"The Lord takes on various forms to carry out
His pastimes, and He was pleased that the
form the Goddess of Fortune had taken was
just right for her to be His consort."*

SRIMAD BHAGAVATAM 10.60.9

Contents

Preface

The stories and narratives of Shri Krishna have fascinated me for many years now. But in the back of my mind, I've always wondered which versions of the stories are correct, which are incorrect, and which actually happened. This past year, two courses I've taken at the University of Mumbai, Vallabh Vedanta and Comparative Mythology, have helped me put this question into perspective. The Vedanta viewpoint is that all of the versions most likely occurred in different Kalpas (Hindu units of time), whilst the Comparative Mythology response is that all of the narratives are sacred to a group of people at different points in time. These perspectives have finally allowed me to be at ease and take joy in the sacred writings.

In this book, I share one of Krishna's stories that caught my imagination. This is compiled from various sources, including the Garga Samhita attributed to the great Garga Muni, Krishna's family priest, Srimad Bhagavata Purana, one of the eighteen great Puranas, and an oral story I heard at a recent traditional Bhagavata Saptah.

The Sacred Love Letter: Krishna weds Rukmini is a story that expands our understanding of culture and tradition while also bringing joy and sparking our imagination.

Happy reading!

Kiran Java

kiran@kiranjava.com

A princess is born

Princess Rukmini was the daughter of King Bheeshmak of the Kingdom of Vidarbha. He was a powerful king who ruled from his capital Kundinapuri. Princess Rukmini was born on the eighth day of the waning moon in the Hindu lunar month of Pausha, which falls in December or January. The day is popularly known as Rukmini Ashtami. Her parents named her after the Sanskrit word Rukhma, which means 'radiant or bright'. Rukmini had a golden yellow complexion and fair hands. Her face was stunning and brighter than the light of 10 million moons. Her hair was braided and tied in a stylish knot. Flowers adorned her hair, and she always carried her favorite lotus flower in her hand. Her mother lavished her with precious ornaments. Rukmini exuded grace and beauty. Many people believed that Rukmini was the incarnation of the goddess Lakshmi, Vishnu's consort.

Throughout her life, she was known by many other lovely names that reflected her characteristics. Names like Shree, which meant Lakshmi, the goddess of fortune; Ruchiranan, the one with a beautiful face like a blooming lotus flower; Vaidarbhi, the one from the Kingdom of Vidarbha; Bhaishmi, the daughter of Bheeshmak; Rakhumai, mother Rukmini; Chiryauvana, the one who is forever young; and Pradyuma Janani, the mother of Pradyumna.

Princess Rukmini had five brothers, the eldest being Rukmi, and the others Rukmarath, Rukmabahu, Rukmakesh, and Rukmamali. Rukmini was the youngest daughter of King Bheeshmak and the only sister of the five brothers.

Rukmi, her eldest brother, was keen to marry his sister to his friend Shishupal. Shishupal was the Prince of Chedi and King Damagosh's son. Shishupal's mother, Srutashubh, was Krishna's father Vasudev's sister, and thus Krishna's aunt.

Rukmini's brother Prince Rukmi, who was an ally of King Jarasandha, opposed Krishna's alliance with his sister. Rukmini's parents, on the other hand, thought Krishna would be a good match for their daughter. However, Rukmi persuaded his father that Shishupal, the crown prince of Chedi and a great warrior, would make a better match for Princess Rukmini.

A love letter for Krishna

When Rukmini came to hear about her betrothal to Shishupal, she made it clear to her parents that she did not wish to marry him. She had heard about the bravery, beauty, and prowess of Krishna from *rishis*, sages, and other visitors to her palace. She had heard about Krishna's many heroic deeds such as the killing of the tyrant Kamsa and standing up to the evil king Jarasandha. She had gradually fallen in love with Krishna and wished to marry him. When she realized that her brother Prince Rukmi had managed to convince her father and her other brothers to give her hand in marriage to Shishupal, she knew that she needed to come up with a plan. She refused to eat, sing to her parrot, or play her musical instruments. Instead, she began writing a long letter to Krishna explaining the situation. She then had it delivered to Krishna in his city of Dwarka by a trusted Brahmin. When the Brahmin arrived in Dwarka, the gatekeepers took him to see Krishna.

Uddhav had come to see his cousin Krishna that day. He was telling him about his journey to Gokul and meeting the residents of Braja. Uddhav was describing the intense devotion they all had for Krishna.

When the Brahmin entered the hall, he couldn't tell the difference between Krishna and Uddhav because they were so similar. Both were tall and handsome, dressed in yellow and wearing exquisite earrings. They welcomed the Brahmin and offered him a seat. By mistake, the Brahmin gave the letter to Uddhav. Krishna smiled and requested that Uddhav read it aloud.

Uddhav complied with his request and read, "O! *Bhuvana-sundara*, most beautiful one in all the worlds, when I heard of your prowess and beauty, my mind was fixed upon you alone." Uddhav was taken aback and turned to Krishna, saying, "This letter is for you, Krishna." He began to hand over the letter to Krishna. Krishna stopped him and said, "Listen Uddhav, I have never done anything that is hidden from anyone. When I was a child, I used to break the pots of the dear *gopis* in front of everyone. When I stole butter, everyone found out. Everyone was aware of my liberating Putana, chastising Kaliya *Naag,* and vanquishing evil demons. Everyone was invited to the *Rasa* dance, which was held in the month of autumn. Now that this letter has arrived, it should be read out loud."

Uddhav nodded and continued reading Princess Rukmini's letter.

"O! *Mukunda*, hearing about your prowess and qualities removes one's grief, and hearing about your beauty fulfills the desire of one's eyes. Nobody can match your beauty, vitality, knowledge, youth, wealth, character, lineage, or influence. Which aristocratic girl from a respectable family would not want you as her husband? As a result, I've chosen only you as my husband. I have *arpita* my *atma* to you and given myself over to you. Please come as soon as possible to accept me as your wife. Let Shishupal not steal what belongs to a hero in the same way that a jackal steals from a lion.

If I have adequately worshipped *Bhagavan* with appropriate sacrifices, ritual methods, charity, pious offerings, and vows, and offered customary worship to the *Devas*, Brahmins, and *Gurus*, then please come and take my hand. I must not be claimed by the son of Damagosh or anyone else but you. Tomorrow, O! *Ajeeta*, O! unconquerable one, you must bring your powerful army and enter Vidarbha. You must crush the armies of Chedi and Magadha, win me with your bravery,

and marry me in the *Rakshasa* style. Just as *Rakshasa* demons kidnap their brides.
You may be wondering how you will reach me without fighting or killing some of my relatives because I will be in the inner chambers of the palace.

I'll share a plan: the bride-to-be travels outside the city limits before the wedding to worship the *Kul Devi*. On such an occasion, it is our family tradition to organize a grand *yatra* in honor of the Goddess Girija. I will be expected to join the procession to visit her temple. *Ambuja Aksha*, O! Lotus-eyed One, great gods like Shiva, the husband of Goddess Uma, desire to wash away their ignorance by bathing in the dust of your lotus feet. If I do not receive your mercy, I will perform such *vratas* and severe penances that my body will become weak and my breath will leave my body."

"This is the message I bring to you, O! *Yadu Deva*," said the Brahmin, after Uddhav finished reading the letter. Now, please do whatever is necessary under these circumstances."

Krishna takes a decision

Krishna understood the special implication of each word the princess of Vidarbha had carefully crafted in her letter. Rukmini had addressed Krishna in Sanskrit as *Bhuvanah Sundara*, which meant not only the most beautiful one but also the source of all beauty. She implied that if she was beautiful, it was because of Lord Krishna's grace, as all beauty comes from him.

Krishna was aware of her use of the words *Mukunda* and *Nara Simha*. This meant that Krishna's face had the soft glow of a Boswellia tree flower while also being tough as a lion amongst men. And because he was as swift and powerful as a lion, she knew Krishna could easily whisk her away from the throng of kings who would be present.

Addressing him as *Ambuja Aksha* (lotus-eyed) indicated that, while Rukmini was suffering from the fire of separation, concentrating on his lotus eyes provided her with temporary relief. Krishna noticed Rukmini's emphasis on her complete surrender to him. A sign that since she had surrendered to him, it was his responsibility to save her from marrying another man. Rukmini demonstrated that she understood that the completion of religious duties was not for material gain but to acquire loving devotion to Krishna.

Krishna was pleased with her letter. He had also heard about Princess Rukmini's beauty, grace, and virtues from Garga Muni. Krishna smiled as he took the Brahmin's hand in his and said, "Princess Rukmini has her mind set on me and has dedicated herself to me. The princess is full of grace and beauty, and I am drawn to her as well. But I know her brother, Prince Rukmi, has opposed our relationship and will never give her hand in mine. So my only option is to fight a battle in order to bring her here, just as a flame is born from the friction of wood against wood."

Saying this, Krishna summoned his charioteer. "Daruka, prepare my chariot, we must depart immediately!" he said. Daruka was Krishna's dependable charioteer. He knew which horses in the stable were the fastest. He yoked the horses Saibya, Sugreev, Meghapushp, and Balahak to the chariot and drew them in front of Krishna. He stepped on the chariot and with his hand pulled the Brahmin onto the chariot. They then rode the chariot toward Vidarbha.

Daruka had chosen well. The horses moved swiftly and they arrived in Vidarbha the next morning. In the distance, they saw Vidarbha's capital city of Kundinapuri which stood within a great fortress of seven *yojanas* in diameter. The fort was encircled by a massive moat overflowing with water like a river swollen by the monsoon. The city, surrounded by a high wall, contained many beautiful palaces with shining golden roofs. There were splendid golden spires and many fluttering flags. Peacocks and other birds flew around the city's gardens.

Wedding preparations in Vidarbha

In Vidarbha, King Bheeshmak was busy with all the arrangements to give his daughter's hand in marriage to Shishupal. He had the main avenues, roads and intersections swept, cleaned, and sprinkled with perfumed water. The entire city was decorated with festoons, arches, and multicolored banners on poles. The citizens were dressed in opulent wear and the fragrance of oud incense filled every home.

King Bheeshmak began the rituals with prayers to his ancestors, the demi-gods, and the Brahmins. He arranged for Brahmins to recite the special mantras for the bride's well-being. The best of the Brahmins were invited to chant appropriate verses from the Rig Veda and the Yajur Veda for her protection. The priests who specialized in the fire sacrifice rituals of the Atharva Veda were summoned to perform appropriate rituals to appease the planets and stars. All the Brahmins received gifts of gold, silver, expensive silk clothes, cows, and sesame seeds mixed with jaggery from King

Bheeshmak. Delectable meals were prepared for all of the Brahmins.

Meanwhile, in the kingdom of Chedi, King Damagosh called expert Brahmins to recite mantras for the prosperity of his son, Shishupal. Shishupal was ritually bathed by the Brahmins and then was elegantly dressed as the bridegroom. They wore him a crown decorated with splendid flowers, necklaces, bracelets, armlets, and crest jewels. He was anointed with sweet fragrances and was greeted with auspicious singing, instrumental music, and a shower of grains. King Damagosh made his way to Kundinapuri, the capital of Vidarbha with his son. They were accompanied by numerous elephants, chariots adorned with gold, and an army of soldiers on horses and foot soldiers.

King Bheeshmak of Vidarbha came to the city's entrance to welcome King Damagosh, the groom, Shishupal, and the other guests. Mridanga drums resounded and dancing girls danced in the welcome area. Bheeshmaka worshipped the kings and gave them woolen shawls. He gifted them ornaments of red coral gathered from the ocean, pearl necklaces, and rare flower fragrances. He personally escorted King Damagosh to a palace he had built for his wedding guests.

Thousands of other kings came as guests of Shishupal including famous kings such as Saalv, Jarasandha, Dantvakra, and Vidurath. Some kings were concerned that Krishna would come and steal Shishupal's bride and so they came with their entire army entourage to fight a battle if necessary.

Meanwhile, Krishna's brother Balaram heard of Krishna's plan to steal Princess Rukmini. Then he learned about the ferocious armies of the various kings that had gathered at Vidarbha to fight Krishna if arrived. Balaram took an instant decision then to go to Vidarbha with his own army of soldiers, horses, elephants, and chariots to support Krishna if a fight erupted.

Rukmini's shringara

Handmaidens were summoned to the palace's inner chambers to bathe and dress the bride-to-be in her wedding finery. They wore the auspicious wedding necklace around her neck and adorned her with numerous jeweled ornaments while the female relatives looked on. There was laughter and joy all around. Princess Rukmini, on the other hand, was unconcerned about her appearance. She was waiting for Krishna anxiously. She wondered if the Brahmin she had sent, along with her letter, had made it to Krishna. "The day is drawing to a close, and by the end of the night, my wedding will take place!" she thought to herself. "Where is lotus-eyed Krishna, and why hasn't the Brahmin messenger returned?" she questioned.

"How unlucky am I," Princess Rukmini lamented, "Perhaps the faultless Krishna does not like me and thus has not come to take me. I feel so unlucky because the Supreme Being does not like me, and Lord Shiva does not like me either. Perhaps Shiva's wife, Uma, also known as Gauri, Girija, and Sati, has turned against me." Tears welled up in her lovely eyes, and she reminded herself that there was still time. The lotus-eyed Rukmini continued to meditate on Krishna's lotus feet. Again and again, she thought of Krishna, who is splendid as a dark monsoon cloud.

Within minutes, there was a commotion at the entrance of the inner chamber, and two handmaidens entered. They informed Princess Rukmini that a learned Brahmin had arrived and wanted to meet her.

Princess Rukmini got up to greet him and being an expert, noted the peaceful movements of the Brahmin and the joyfulness on his face. She immediately knew that he brought good news and she smiled.

The Brahmin announced that Krishna had arrived and also told her of his promise to marry her. Princess Rukmini was overjoyed to hear this news. She didn't have anything on hand to gift the Brahmin and could only humbly bow to him.

Krishna's arrival

King Bheeshmak of Vidarbha was overjoyed when he learned that Krishna and Balaram had arrived to witness his daughter's wedding. He personally went to greet them both, carrying beautiful silk clothes, trays of sweets, and other gifts. He offered them many *mangal-patras*, sweet fragrances, and jewels. Accompanied by sweet singing and instrumental music, King Bheeshmak appropriately received Krishna and Balaram. Seeing the beauty and prowess of Krishna he thought to himself, "Alas! I regret that I did not give my daughter Rukmini's hand in marriage to Krishna". King Bheeshmak was gracious and provided suitable lodging for Krishna and Balaram, their entourage, and their armies. In this manner, he made it clear that they were welcome in Vidarbha.

The people of Vidarbha rushed to meet Krishna when they heard he had arrived. They stayed for a long time, catching glimpses of Krishna. Many residents believed that Princess Rukmini would be the best wife for

Krishna and that nobody else could fill the role.

At the same time, they all agreed that Krishna, with his flawless beauty, was the most suitable husband for their princess. "May Krishna, the creator of the three worlds, be pleased with the good deeds and auspicious work we have done and show his mercy by taking the hand of Princess Rukmini," they suddenly wished. They made this wish out of pure love for their princess and Krishna.

Rukmini's visit to the temple of Bhavani

Rukmini left the inner chambers of the palace to walk to the temple of Bhavani. There she would offer her traditional respects as expected of a bride. But as she walked the path, her mind was preoccupied with thoughts about Krishna. She was accompanied by the elder women of the family, her mother, and her aunts as well as her friends. The palace guards protected her and her entourage as they made their way to the temple. Foot soldiers carrying sharpened swords were positioned throughout the area. Other soldiers with upraised weapons rode horses, chariots, and elephants.

Instruments such as the *panavas*, cymbals, drums, and conch shells could be heard in the background. As the *bheri*, *mridanga*, and *dundubhi* drums sounded, expert vocalists, sang sweet songs, poets recited poetry, and dancing girls gracefully danced. Every few minutes auspicious loud calls of "Victory!" resounded. The

Brahmin wives accompanying them were dressed in their traditional finery. They sang melodious songs and chanted appropriate religious verses. They carried valuable jewels, expensive clothes, perfumes, and garlands as gifts. Thousands of maidens trailed behind them carrying trays of precious gifts to be offered to the deity. Bands of musicians, singers, bards, and chroniclers accompanied the entourage.

When Princess Rukmini arrived at the temple of Gauri, she washed her hands and feet and drank the water for purification. Thus sanctified she came in the presence of the goddess. The goddess Bhavani appeared alongside her consort, Lord Shiva. The wives of the Brahmins were experts at the rituals and guided Princess Rukmini in performing the appropriate worship of the goddess.

Princess Rukmini prayed silently, "O, goddess Ambani, wife of Lord Shiva, I repeatedly offer my obeisances to you, please grant my wish, please make Lord Krishna my husband."

She then worshipped the goddess in the appropriate manner. She lit an array of wick lamps and worshipped her with water, fragrances, whole grains, incense, clothing, garlands, necklaces, and jewelry. She then bowed down to the deity.

Each of the married Brahmin women who accompanied the princess worshipped Gauri in the same way. They also offered folded betel nut leaves, sacred threads, fruit, and sugarcane juice. After the rituals, the princess bowed down to the fortunate women and worshiped them with many ornaments and other gifts, before breaking her vow of silence. The women too presented many gifts to Princess Rukmini as *prasad* from the deity. They also blessed her by saying, "May you be beautiful like Shatrupa. May you be virtuous like the goddess Parvati. May you have a faithful husband as Arudhnati has. May you be forgiving like Sita. May you be fortunate like Dakshina. May you be glorious like Indra's wife, Sachi. May you be learned like Saraswati. May you be devoted to your husband as the saintly devotees are devoted to Lord Hari."

Then Princess Rukmini's maidservants assisted her in leaving the temple.

Rukmini glimpses Krishna

As Princess Rukmini walked, she appeared to be the divine power of the Lord, capable of enchanting even the most solemn and serious men. Her hips were adorned with a jewel-studded belt, her breasts were just budding, and her eyes shone. Her face was as radiant as the moonlight. Her jasmine teeth reflected the glow of her ruby-red lips as she smiled sweetly. Tinkling anklets adorned her feet as she walked gracefully like a swan bird. Her grace and beauty astounded the assembled kings. They gazed upon her divine beauty, her shapely waist and face adorned with glittering earrings. Her shy glances and lovely smile astounded them. Some fell unconscious from their elephants, chariots, and horses and their weapons fell to the ground.

Princess Rukmini had dressed beautifully for the procession to worship the deity, but it was only for Krishna. As she walked away from the temple, her eyes searched for Krishna. She delicately moved her hair away from her face and looked at the kings in front of her from the corner of her eyes. Suddenly the princess caught sight of Krishna atop his chariot. His chariot was emblazoned with the Garuda emblem. Their eyes met and Krishna was beaming. Riding on a chariot fast as the wind, pulled by the best of horses, and driven by Daruka, Krishna left his army, cut apart the opposing army, and raced to the cluster of women as the wind enters a forest. As his enemies looked on, he gently scooped up Princess Rukmini and placed her on his chariot. Again and again, Krishna twanged his Saranga bow, the best of weapons, and, as the demigods looked on, kidnapped beautiful Princess Rukmini.

As the other kings looked on, Krishna pushed forward, driving back the kings who had gathered around his chariot and returned to his army. When he returned to his own army, the demigods and the Yadavas sounded drums of victory. Balaram rode his chariot blocking the other kings. Krishna exited the circle like a lion removing his prey from a pack of jackals. The demigods, *siddhas*, and their young daughters showered flowers upon Krishna's chariot.

The kings, who were led by King Jarasandha were fiercely hostile to Krishna. Krishna's deed had humiliated them all. "We are mighty archers, and some mere cowherd boys have stolen our honor, just as tiny animals might steal the honor of lions!" they exclaimed.

Battle of the kings

The kings supporting Shishupal wore their armor and mounted their steeds to chase after Krishna. When the commanders of the Yadava army saw the kings following them, they turned around and prepared to string their bows with sharp arrows. The kings were on fast horses, shoulders of elephants, or seated upon swift chariots. They aimed rows of arrows at the Yadava army from their respective steeds, just as clouds rained on mountains.

Rukmini became terrified when she saw Krishna's army covered in sharp arrows. She looked at Krishna, her eyes filled with fear. Krishna smiled as he noticed her staring at him. "O one with beautiful eyes, don't be afraid. The enemy force will soon be vanquished by your soldiers," he said.

Krishna's army led by Gada and Sankarshan was enraged by the arrogance of the kings and rained arrows on their horses, elephants, and chariots. Many enemy soldiers were killed. They were beheaded by Krishna's army. The battlefield was strewn with severed body parts. There were heads donning helmets, earrings, or turbans, legs, fingerless hands, and hands clutching swords, clubs, and bows. The severed heads of battle animals such as horses, elephants, donkeys, camels, and wild asses were scattered throughout the area.

When their armies were defeated by the Yadavas, the kings, led by King Jarasandha, became distraught and began fleeing the battle. They all went to meet Shishupal. They saw Shishupal's complexion had lost its color. He appeared depressed and all his enthusiasm had vanished.

King Jarasandha addressed Shishupal, "O tiger amongst men, do not despair and get depressed. The truth is that happiness and unhappiness are not eternal. Humans are controlled by time, just as a puppet is controlled by the puppeteer and dances to the whims of the puppeteer. Sorrow and happiness are natural components of life." King Jarasandha explained that he and his twenty-three armies had lost seventeen battles and won only once against Krishna. "But I never lament or rejoice because I know that we are ruled by time and fate," King Jarasandha said. "We can clearly see that, despite the fact that we are all commanders of great military armies, we have been defeated by the Yadavas and their small entourage, who are protected by Krishna," Jarasandha added. Because time is on their side, our adversaries have conquered us this time. However, when the time is on our side, we shall defeat our enemy.

Thus enlightened by King Jarasandha and his other friends, Shishupal prepared his entourage to return to his kingdom of Chedi. All the other kings who had survived the battle also returned to their respective kingdoms.

Rukmi fights Krishna

Rukmi, on the other hand, was enraged that Krishna had kidnapped his sister and planned to marry her in the Rakshasa manner. He was opposed to their marriage from the start, preferring his friend Shishupal to marry his sister Princess Rukmini. He vowed in front of all the kings that he would pursue Krishna, fight and defeat him, and reclaim his sister. He vowed that unless he defeated Krishna, he would not return to his kingdom of Vidarbha or set foot in its capital, Kundinapuri. He pursued Krishna with all of his military might in order to reclaim his sister.

Rukmi dressed in his metallic armor and gathered all his weapons. Wielding his bow, he commanded his charioteer, "Ride the chariot immediately to where Krishna is now. I shall battle with Krishna to get my sister back. Krishna is a cowherd boy with a wicked mind. His strength has gotten to his head and he has abducted my sister. Today I will shoot my sharp arrows at him and teach him a lesson".

Boasting foolishly and ignorant of the true identity and extent of the power of Krishna, Rukmi challenged him to a duel. "Come fight me, Krishna," he yelled from his lone chariot. Rukmi twanged his bow with a thunderous sound and shot three sharp iron arrows at Krishna. "Stand here, you cowherd boy," he shouted. He threw insults at Krishna, "You have stolen my sister like a crow steals sacrificial butter, you are a coward, Krishna, you are a cheater, a fool, and full of false pride. Release my sister before I strike you with more arrows and knock you down".

Krishna smiled in response to Rukmi's anger. Quietly and swiftly he pulled out a single arrow and cut Rukmi's bow in two just as knowledge cuts the darkness of repeated birth and death. In the next second, Krishna aimed eight arrows striking all four of Rukmi's horses. Krishna tied up Rukmi's charioteer with two arrows and brought down Rukmi's flag atop his chariot with three arrows.

Rukmi was not about to give up. He grabbed another bow and shot five arrows at Krishna. The arrows struck Krishna's armor and fell to the ground like flower petals. Krishna took six arrows and shot them in Rukmi's direction. The arrows shattered Rukmi's bow. Rukmi took out another bow but Krishna broke it before he could prepare it. Rukmi pulled out an iron mace, a three-pointed spear, a sword and shield, a long thrusting spear, and a javelin; but one by one Krishna smashed all of them to pieces.

Rukmi then leaped from his chariot and charged at Krishna with his sword, as a bird flies into the wind. Krishna deftly shattered his sword into a hundred pieces without harming Rukmi. He then took his sharp knife and aimed it at Rukmi. When Princess Rukmini saw Krishna about to kill her brother, she screamed and fell at Krishna's feet. She sobbed at Krishna's feet, begging him to save her brother. "O controller of all powers, mighty-armed one, master of the universe, and lord of lords, please spare the life of my brother Rukmi," she cried.

Rukmini's eyes welled up with tears, her throat became dry and she trembled with fear. She choked up with grief and tightly clutched the lotus feet of Krishna. Krishna looked down at the princess with compassion and withdrew his knife. He shot an arrow with a rope tying Rukmi's hands like a prisoner. He shaved Rukmi's hair and mustache with his sword, leaving tufts of hair on his face and head. Meanwhile, Krishna's Yadav army crushed Rukmi's armed forces like an elephant trampling lotus flowers.

Balaram's words of wisdom

When the Yadava clan approached Krishna, they saw Rukmi in such a terrible condition. Balaram was moved by his situation and filled with compassion. Turning toward Krishna he said, "To disfigure a close relative by shaving off his mustache and hair is as good as killing him. Why kill him again when he has already been killed by the sins he has committed?". Saying this, Balaram released Rukmi from the ropes and set him free.

"O! *Saadhvi*, Please don't be upset with us for how we have treated your brother Rukmi," Balaram said to Princess Rukmini. Prince Rukmi is solely to blame for his predicament. The Supreme Being's illusionary powers cause us to forget who we truly are and begin to identify with this physical body. The thought that someone is a friend, someone else is a neutral party, and someone else is an enemy is an illusion created by *prakriti* or material nature. This material body is composed of matter, senses, and three *gunas* or modes of nature. The body is responsible for the suffering of the cycle of birth and death. The confused or ignorant perceive the one Supreme Being manifested in many bodies as many and different, just as the light of the celestial bodies in the sky is perceived as different."

The body causes us to suffer the cycle of birth and death. Then he added, "O intelligent lady, know that the soul never has any contact with nor is separated from the material objects for the soul is the originator or the source. It is like the sun which doesn't have contact with what is seen or the sense of sight nor is it separated from it. Birth and transformations are experienced by the physical body, never by the soul. Therefore, O princess I hope this divine knowledge dispels the grief that clouds your mind and that you once again regain your original composure and smile.

Thus enlightened by Balaram, the beautiful Princess Rukmini was able to set aside her despair, calm her mind through scriptural knowledge, and regain her composure.

The wedding

All the kings had been defeated by Krishna. After being defeated, Prince Rukmi lost all his strength. He could not forget his humiliation at the hands of Krishna. Because he had vowed never to return to his capital city without his younger sister, he did not return to Kundinapuri. Instead, he settled in a large city he built, which he named Bhojakata.

Thus vanquishing all his enemies, Krishna brought Princess Rukmini, the daughter of King Bheeshmak to his kingdom of Dwarka. Amidst great fanfare, all of Dwarka's citizens rejoiced at the news. Krishna was their beloved chief and King. They were excited to meet their new future queen.

In the month of Margashirsha (November-December), there was a great festival in Dwarka city as Krishna married beautiful-faced Rukmini. The city was beautifully decorated. Tall festive columns and archways were festooned with flowers. Velvet and gold embroidered banners and precious stones were hung over doorways. Decorated water pots, lamps, and burning *aguru*-scented incense were placed outside every home.

Krishna and Rukmini were married according to the holy wedding rituals prescribed in the Vedic tradition. All the men, women, and children of Dwarka were invited to grace the occasion. They dressed in silk attires and wore glittering jewels and earrings. They brought wedding gifts, which they respectfully presented to the groom and bride.

Krishna and Rukmini's wedding drew guests from various kingdoms all over the country. The royal families of the Kuru, Kaikeya, Vidarbha, Yadu, and Kunti clans were all present in force. Their elephants cleansed the streets with perfumed water. They enhanced the beauty of the city by placing trunks of the auspicious plantain tree and betel nut on all of Dwarka's doorways.

The story of Rukmini's sacred love letter and her marriage to Krishna was eulogized in song. Their glories were sung throughout the lands. Kings and queens, as well as their sons and daughters, were surprised and astonished to hear the tale of Krishna's feat. It filled everyone who heard it with unfathomable joy and bliss. For this was no ordinary story. It was the story of the lord of opulence uniting with the goddess of fortune.

Meeting The Kathak Rishi: A Brief Interaction With Mahamahopadhyaya Dr. Puru Dadheech's Kathak Research

This is a very short read that describes my tryst with Kathak classical dance and its Shastras, how I met Mahamahopadyay Dr. Puru Dadheech, and the doors to a wonderful world that opened up. This short read contains excerpts from my previously published articles about Mahamahopadyay Dr. Puru Dadheech's work that have been enjoyed by readers. These are but a few pearls from the ocean of knowledge that have been researched and shared by Mahamahopadhyay Dr. Puru Dadheech and my interaction with his research. If you are a reader who takes joy in reading about Kathak or are curious about its Shastras then this short read is for you.

Notes

Kiran Java

Kiran Java is the author of 'Meeting the Kathak Rishi', #1 hot new release in the US. She is known for her sacred writings and articles on Kathak classical dance. She has written for various national and international media. She is curator-editor at Pushtimarg Studies and host of 'Krishna Stories with Kiran Java' Podcast.

She has a Masters degree in Journalism and Communication and a B.Sc. degree in Marketing from Eastern Connecticut State University, USA. She has a certification in Vallabh Vedanta from Mumbai University and is pursuing a Post Graduate Diploma in Comparative Mythology.

She holds a Diploma in Natyashastra with Kathak relevancy under Dr. Puru Dadheech and has learned Kathak classical dance under Dr. Nandkishore Kapote. She has learned Haveli Sangeet under Pt. B.P. Gandharva and has released a few singles.